Polish Americans

Dale Anderson

Consultant: Dr. Mieczyslaw B. B. Biskupski,
S. A. Blejwas Chair in Polish History, Central Connecticut State University

Curriculum Consultant: Michael Koren,
Social Studies Teacher, Maple Dale School, Fox Point, Wisconsin

WORLD ALMANAC® LIBRARY

Please visit our web site at: www.garethstevens.com
For a free color catalog describing World Almanac® Library's
list of high-quality books and multimedia programs,
call 1-800-848-2928 (USA) or 1-800-387-3178 (Canada).
World Almanac® Library's fax: (414) 332-3567.

Library of Congress Cataloging-in-Publication Data

Anderson, Dale, 1953–
    Polish Americans / by Dale Anderson.
        p. cm. – (World Almanac Library of American immigration)
    Includes bibliographical references and index.
    ISBN-10: 0-8368-7317-3 – ISBN-13: 978-0-8368-7317-7 (lib. bdg.)
    ISBN-10: 0-8368-7330-0 – ISBN-13: 978-0-8368-7330-6 (softcover)
    1. Polish Americans–History–Juvenile literature.   2. Polish Americans–
Social conditions–Juvenile literature.   3. Immigrants–United States–History–
Juvenile literature.   4. Poland–Emigration and immigration–History–Juvenile
literature.   5. United States–Emigration and immigration–History–Juvenile
literature.   I. Title.   II. Series.
    E184.P7A53   2007   4230
    973'.0049185–dc22   2006005390

First published in 2007 by
World Almanac® Library
A member of the WRC Media Family of Companies
330 West Olive Street, Suite 100
Milwaukee, WI 53212, USA

Produced by Discovery Books
Editor: Jacqueline Laks Gorman and Sabrina Crewe
Designer and page production: Sabine Beaupré
Photo researcher: Sabrina Crewe
Maps and diagrams: Stefan Chabluk
World Almanac® Library editorial direction: Mark J. Sachner
World Almanac® Library editor: Carol Ryback
World Almanac® Library art direction: Tammy West
World Almanac® Library production: Jessica Morris

Picture credits: Chicago Historical Society: 28; CORBIS: cover, 5, 11, 13, 17, 18, 19,
31, 34, 39, 43; Getty Images: 10, 37, 38; Institute of Texan Cultures, University
of Texas at San Antonio: title page, 20–21, 27, 32; Library of Congress: 7, 8, 15, 16,
29, 33; National Park Service: 22, 23; Sabine Beaupré: 42; United States Holocaust
Memorial Museum, courtesy of Instytut Pamieci Narodowej: 9.

Printed in the United States of America

1 2 3 4 5 6 7 8 9 10 09 08 07 06

Contents

Front cover: Poles and Polish Americans observe feast days and holidays with traditional costumes and folk dances. These girls, in costumes that reflect the colors of the Polish flag, wait to perform at a Polish festival in New Jersey.

Title page: Some of the first Polish Americans to come to the United States in the 1800s settled in Texas. These settlers in Bandera, Texas, in the early 1900s worked at their family molasses mill.

Introduction

The United States has often been called "a nation of immigrants." With the exception of Native Americans—who have inhabited North America for thousands of years—all Americans can trace their roots to other parts of the world.

Immigration is not a thing of the past. More than seventy million people came to the United States between 1820 and 2005. One-fifth of that total—about fourteen million people—immigrated since the start of 1990. Overall, more people have immigrated permanently to the United States than to any other single nation.

Push and Pull

Historians write of the "push" and "pull" factors that lead people to emigrate. "Push" factors are the conditions in the homeland that convince people to leave. Many immigrants to the United States were—and still are—fleeing persecution or poverty. "Pull" factors are those that attract people to settle in another country. The dream of freedom or jobs or both continues to pull immigrants to the United States. People from many countries around the world view the United States as a place of opportunity.

Building a Nation

Immigrants to the United States have not always found what they expected. People worked long hours for little pay, often doing jobs that others did not want to do. Many groups also endured prejudice.

"In America you can reach your dreams. This is not a privilege for a select few, but a goal reachable by all. The United States gives people a chance to fulfill their needs in education, travel, culture, and all the things that are so much more important than material goods. . . . The feeling of freedom here is not just theoretical. It's a normal way of life."

Andrzej Nowak, who came from Poland in 1986, on the opportunities of life in the United States

In spite of these challenges, immigrants and their children built the United States of America, from its farms, railroads, and computer industries to its beliefs and traditions. They have enriched American life with their culture and ideas. Although they honor their heritage, most immigrants and their descendants are proud to call themselves Americans first and foremost.

Immigrants from Poland

The number of people who left Poland for the United States over the years is difficult to determine. Poland was occupied by other nations for many years, and during this time U.S. officials did not record Poland as a place of origin. It included Polish immigrants in its numbers for immigrants from Austria-Hungary, Germany, and Russia. Complicating matters further, not all immigrants who came from Poland were ethnic Poles. Some were Ukrainians, Germans, Lithuanians, Jews, or members of other groups.

▲ During the great wave of immigration between 1870 and 1924, many Poles arrived at the immigration station on Ellis Island in New York Harbor. This young Polish man arrived in 1907.

From American colonial times to the late 1800s, a few Polish individuals and scattered groups of Poles came to the United States. The great wave of Polish immigration occurred between 1870 and 1924, when, experts say, about 1.8 million Poles crossed the Atlantic Ocean. After World War II, immigration from Poland slowed to a trickle, but the United States admitted about 253,000 Poles who had suffered special hardship in the war. From 1971 to 2004, almost 350,000 Poles made the journey. These immigrants and their descendants built a new community in the United States, a Polish American community they call *Polonia*.

CHAPTER 1

Life in the Homeland

oles are Slavs, related to the peoples who settled Russia, Ukraine, and nearby lands. Centuries ago, Poles created a kingdom that for many years was a powerful presence in Europe. Unlike other Slavs—who were mostly Eastern Orthodox Christians—the great majority of Poles became Roman Catholics. Their religion made them culturally closer to Western Europeans than to Eastern Europeans.

Polish history in the last three hundred years was shaped by several factors. First, the country was surrounded by larger and more powerful neighbors who threatened its existence. This helped intensify Poles' feelings of patriotism. Second, for many Poles, membership in the Catholic Church was a vital part of being Polish. Poland was also known for its religious tolerance, however, and it was home to a significant minority of Jews and other ethnic groups. Third, in the 1700s and 1800s, Polish society, like that

◀ Poland sits on the south shore of the Baltic Sea. For a small part of its long and distinguished history, Poland was occupied by Germany, Austria, and Russia. This map shows Poland's boundaries as they are today.

The Black Madonna

Polish Catholics revere the Black Madonna of Czestochowa, a painting of Mary holding her son, Jesus, both with faces blackened by soot from prayer candles. The work is believed to be a portrait of Mary painted by Saint Luke, author of one of the books of the New Testament. In 1382, tradition says, a Polish prince was bringing the painting home when the cart carrying it could not be moved past the town of Czestochowa, Poland. Convinced that this event was a sign from heaven, the prince built a church and monastery to house the painting. It has remained there ever since, an object of deep devotion for Catholic Poles. In 1966, Polish Americans finished building a church dedicated to the Black Madonna in the city of Doylestown, Pennsylvania, and placed a copy of the painting there.

of other European countries, was made up of a small number of landowning nobles and a large mass of poor peasants who worked the farmland and had little education or money and few rights.

Carving Up the Country

By the late 1700s, Poland was much weaker than its neighbors, Prussia (which later became Germany), Russia, and Austria. In 1772, those countries began the first of three partitions of Poland, in which each seized Polish land. After the partition of 1793, a soldier named Tadeusz Kosciuszko led a revolt against the Russians. The rebels were defeated, and in 1795, the three powers took control of remaining Polish land. At that point, Poland ceased to exist as an independent country.

Polish patriots did not give up the fight, however, and revolted

▶ St. Alexander's in Warsaw, Poland, was one of several huge churches that dominated the city. The Roman Catholic Church has been an important influence on Poles and Polish American culture.

Ignacy Paderewski (1860–1941)

In the late 1800s, classical pianist Ignacy Paderewski gained great fame for his powerful playing style and showy performances. Paderewski was also devoted to the cause of Polish independence. During World War I, his pleadings helped convince U.S. president Woodrow Wilson to support that cause. Paderewski was chosen to head the new Polish government that was formed to lead the nation. His term in office was brief, however. Disliking the criticism he received, he resigned in less than a year. Paderewski began performing in concerts again, donating the profits to civilians hurt by the war. When Germany invaded Poland in 1939, launching World War II, Paderewski joined the Polish government-in-exile.

several more times. All of these revolts failed, causing the emigration of a number of political exiles. A few of these exiles went to the United States in the early 1830s and late 1840s.

While the struggle for independence continued, the lives of Poland's peasants went on as before. Their days were filled with hard work—plowing, planting, weeding, and harvesting fields—and they had few legal rights. The landowners sometimes treated peasants harshly. The occupying powers of Prussia, Russia, and Austria, meanwhile, tried to suppress the Polish language and culture and forced males to fight in their armies. These frustrations led some Poles to emigrate to the United States in the 1850s. Political and economic frustrations also spurred much larger numbers of people to emigrate in later years, from the 1870s to the early 1920s.

Free Poland

The dream of independence was finally realized in 1918, when World War I ended. The United States, Britain, and France had defeated Germany and Austria. Russia, meanwhile, had collapsed in a revolution that eventually put communists in control of the country they renamed the Soviet Union. The victorious countries agreed in 1919 to recognize an independent Poland. Thousands of people who had left Poland returned after independence, while others emigrated. About a quarter of a million people left Poland for the United States in the first few years after the war.

Poland in World War II

Poland's freedom did not last long. Adolf Hitler rose to power in Germany in 1933 and made plans to conquer Europe, starting with Poland. In August 1939, he signed a secret agreement with the Soviet Union to divide Poland after conquering it. On September 1, 1939, Germany invaded Poland, and Soviet forces soon moved in from the east. Poland held out bravely for some weeks, but was defeated by mid-October. When Hitler turned on his ally and invaded the Soviet Union in 1941, all of Poland wound up in German hands.

Those hands were cruel. The Germans rounded up and killed more than three million Polish Jews, reducing a once large

"The Germans used to bomb systematically. . . . At seven o'clock in the morning they would start, and they would first finish the corner house. Fifteen minutes later they would finish the next one, then the next one, then the next one . . . until they finished [destroying] the whole block, with heavy artillery. . . . Eventually . . . you could stand on one side of Warsaw and you could see the other end. There was hardly anything left."

Polish immigrant Wojtek Pobog, remembering the German destruction of Warsaw during World War II

▼ German guards march Polish Jews out of the ghetto in Krakow, Poland, in 1943. The people are being taken to one of the concentration camps where millions of Jews were killed during World War II.

▲ Members of the Polish Home Army prepare to fight in Warsaw, Poland, in a famous uprising against the German occupation in 1944. The resistance fighters are wearing captured German uniforms with armbands striped red and white for the Polish flag.

population to a fragment. About two million Polish Catholic civilians were killed as well. The Poles, however, formed a large and brave resistance movement in which tens of thousands valiantly fought the Germans.

In 1945, Germany was defeated. Along with several million dead, Poland had suffered terrible destruction. Another quarter of a million Poles emigrated to the United States in the wake of WWII. Many were civilians who had lost their homes; others were Poles who had fought the Germans.

The Rise and Fall of Communism

After Germany's defeat, Soviet troops moved into Poland. Soviet leader Joseph Stalin wanted to install communist governments in Poland and other nations in eastern Europe. By 1947, communists ruled Poland, and leaders of opposing parties fled the country.

For the next forty years, the government controlled all aspects of life in Poland. A struggling economy and restrictions led many Poles to want to leave the country. Between 1950 and the late 1980s, nearly 185,000 Poles came to the United States. It was not easy to get government permission, and some waited a long time for a passport allowing them to travel.

Late in 1978, Polish cardinal Karol Wojtyla was elected pope—the head of the Roman Catholic Church. Taking the name

"[They hoped] to escape from a country in which one's life was constantly threatened; where a peaceful life, with even minimal freedom to develop intellectually, culturally, and economically, was blocked."

Sociologist Theresita Polzin, writing in the 1980s about people who left communist Poland

John Paul II, he traveled to Poland in 1979 and inspired Poles with his message that the nation should be free of communist rule and Soviet domination. In 1980, a protest movement arose in Poland, and workers across the country formed an independent union called Solidarity to push for economic and political changes. Lech Walesa, who rose from shipyard worker to become Poland's most prominent labor activist, led Solidarity. The government struck back the next year, outlawing Solidarity and declaring martial law. Although Walesa and other Solidarity leaders were imprisoned, the movement continued in secret.

Solidarity had an influential ally in Pope John Paul II. Throughout the 1980s, he worked behind the scenes to convince Polish leaders to legalize Solidarity again.

By the end of the 1980s, Poland's communist leaders decided to make changes. In 1989, they allowed free and fair elections. Walesa's commitment and bravery, meanwhile, had attracted the attention of the world. Solidarity members won many seats in the new legislature, and the next year Walesa became the nation's president. These changes helped spur the collapse of communism across eastern Europe and even in the Soviet Union.

▲ Former Polish president Lech Walesa visited New York City in 2005 during celebrations for the twenty-fifth anniversary of Solidarity. Walesa stands before the January 5, 1982, cover image of TIME magazine, on which he is named "Man of the Year."

Life in Poland after communism was not easy. Poles faced the challenge of reforming the government and the economy, finding jobs for workers, cleaning up polluting factories, and providing health care and other services. Progress came slowly but steadily, and the Poles now have the satisfaction of knowing that they finally control their own nation.

Traditional Culture in Rural Societies

For centuries, Poland was a rural, farm-based society. Many of the customs that continued in the U.S. were shaped by seasonal rhythms tied to farming practices. Spring was marked by the tradition of Dyngus, which involved sprinkling or pouring water on a person's head. The tradition symbolized a cleansing and renewal linked with the new farming year. Dozynki, celebrated at the end of the farming year, marked the end of the harvest and included music, dancing, and feasting.

Village-wide activities were common in rural societies. In some parts of Poland, custom required inviting everyone in the village—without exception—to weddings. Sometimes, groups of people from these same villages or regions emigrated together to the United States.

"Poland, where I was born, was a wonderful place, the land was fertile, different kinds of wild fruits grew, and taking everything into consideration, the people were happy but for the most part very poor. My parents were likewise poor. However, they seemed to find time to tell stories and laugh."

Stanley A. Kula, born in Tarnow, Poland, who came to the United States and settled in Columbus, Nebraska, in 1897

Polish Catholic Customs

Polish Catholics observe several religious holidays and feasts, with the two most important coming at Christmas and Easter. Traditionally, Christmas centered on the *wigilia* on Christmas Eve, a special meal of several meatless dishes that women spent the entire day cooking. The table was decorated with hay, to symbolize the manger in which Jesus was born, and a white cloth, representing Mary. Before eating, family members broke off pieces of the *oplatek*, a flat wafer decorated with Christmas patterns. Sharing the wafer demonstrated forgiveness and good wishes. After the feast, the Poles sang carols, exchanged gifts, and went to midnight mass at the local church.

▲ Poles and Polish Americans observe feast days and holidays with traditional dance and costumes. These girls are waiting to perform at a Polish festival in New Jersey.

Folk Arts

Egg decorating was, and still is, popular around Easter, and Poles often ask priests to bless the decorated eggs before eating them. Other Polish folk arts include wood carving, paper cutting, and fine needlework. Some of that needlework shows up in the colorful folk costumes people wear on special occasions. A dazzling variety of colors and styles originate from about sixty distinct regions of Poland. Regions had their own folk dances as well—Polish dancing is honored all over the world and is popular in the United States.

Music and Literature

Poland is well known for the artistic and intellectual achievements of its people. The country has produced many masters of literature, music, and the arts. Four Polish writers—including novelist Henryk Sienkiewicz and poet Czeslaw Milosz—have won the Nobel Prize for Literature. Milosz lived many years in the United States after leaving communist Poland. Frederic Chopin, who lived in the 1800s, was a brilliant pianist as a child and developed into one of the greatest composers of piano music. Many of his works are based on Polish folk dances. Ignacy Paderewski, Artur Rubinstein, and others have carried on the great tradition of Polish piano music.

CHAPTER 2

Emigration

Conditions in Poland persuaded more than two million Poles to come to the United States over the past two centuries or so. Those who came before 1850 and between 1950 and 1990 left Poland largely for political reasons. The great bulk of Polish immigrants—those who came between 1850 and the early 1920s—were mostly seeking a better economic life, although political struggles were a factor, too.

Early Emigrants

The earliest Polish emigrants mostly traveled alone or in small groups. Their decisions to leave Poland were mainly personal. Tadeusz Kosciuszko and Kazimierz Pulaski were Polish nobles who came in the 1770s to help American colonists in their fight for independence from Britain. Pulaski and Kosciuszko's efforts gave Americans a strong positive impression of the Polish people.

Tadeusz Kosciuszko (1746–1817)

A Polish patriot and lover of freedom, Tadeusz Kosciuszko was serving in the Polish army when the American Revolution began. Thrilled by the cause of liberty, he crossed the Atlantic to fight with the American colonists. Kosciuszko served in the Continental Army from 1776 to the end of the Revolution in 1783. He helped win the key Battle of Saratoga in 1777 and designed the fortifications for the U.S. fort at West Point, New York. After returning to Poland, Kosciuszko fought against the Russians. Captured after his failed revolt in 1794, he spent two years in a Russian prison before being released and returning to the United States. When another attempt to free Poland from foreign control failed, he retired to Switzerland in frustration. The U.S. Congress had granted Kosciuszko some land in gratitude for his role in the American Revolution. In his will, he directed that the land be sold and the money used to free African American slaves and to help set up a school for former slaves.

▸ Two early Polish emigrants, the war heroes Kazimierz Pulaski and Tadeusz Kosciuszko, came to America to help Americans fight for independence. The two were later featured on this 1917 poster encouraging Poles in the United States to fight for Poland in World War I.

Polacy! Kościuszko i Pułaski walczyli za wolność Polski i innych narodów! Idźmy w ich ślady! Hej na bój z wrogiem odwiecznym Polski i wolności!

POLES! KOSCIUSZKO AND PULASKI FOUGHT FOR THE LIBERTY OF POLAND AND OTHER NATIONS. FOLLOW THEIR EXAMPLE. ENLIST IN THE POLISH ARMY!

The hope of ridding Poland of foreign control remained strong in Poland, and nobles and intellectuals took up the cause. Some staged a significant revolt in 1830–1831. The revolt failed, and leading members were arrested by Austrian authorities. Austria eventually gave the patriots the choice of returning to Russian-held Poland or being sent into exile in the United States. The 234 patriots who chose exile came in 1834, forming the first significant movement of Polish emigrants to the United States. A few hundred more exiles came after another failed revolution in 1848.

Seeking Better Lives

Beginning around 1850, a new fervor drove Polish emigration: the desire for better lives. The exiles who had emigrated in previous years had been educated and cultured people. This new surge of emigrants, which turned into a massive wave beginning in 1870, consisted mostly of peasants who hoped that moving to a new land would mean increased opportunites for an easier life.

Many Poles who came to the United States did not plan to stay. They planned to work for a few years, earn and save money, and

The Cost of Emigration

The availability of cheap passage across the Atlantic Ocean on steamships was one spur to the great migration from eastern and southern Europe that lasted from 1870 to the mid-1920s. Price wars among different steamship lines helped emigrants by keeping ticket prices low. Steamships could hold far more people than earlier sailing ships, and steamship companies were happy to take large numbers of immigrants to fill their holds. In addition, the use of steam power shortened the journey from months to weeks.

return to Poland to buy land and live more comfortably there. Many did indeed return, but not usually because they succeeded in gaining financial security. The majority returned home because they missed their families and homeland or because they could not adjust to the different ways of life.

The Great Migration

In the great migration from 1870 to the mid-1920s, most Poles boarded ships in the port cities of Bremen or Hamburg, Germany.

▲ The port of Hamburg, Germany, in 1873. Many emigrants, including Poles, left Europe by ship from Hamburg.

First, however, emigrants had to get the necessary papers to make a legal entry into the United States. Then, they made the overland journey to the port, most traveling there by cart or train.

The Hamburg-Amerika complex in Hamburg (built by a German shipping company, the Hamburg-Amerika Line) was huge and could house about four thousand people at a time. It was also well organized. Large kitchens prepared food as travelers waited for their ship to leave. Travelers received medical inspections in which officials looked for evidence of infectious diseases. Hopeful emigrants were rejected if medical officials decided they were too sick to travel.

▲ A group of Polish and Russian steerage passengers gathered on deck during a journey to the United States in the early 1900s.

On the day of departure, passengers crowded onto the ships. The great mass of immigrants was too poor to afford cabins. They were sent below the decks to the steerage section. Conditions there were awful. Males and females were placed in separate areas, splitting families. Furnishings were limited to bunk beds. Toilets were shared by large numbers of people. The rooms inside the ships were hot,

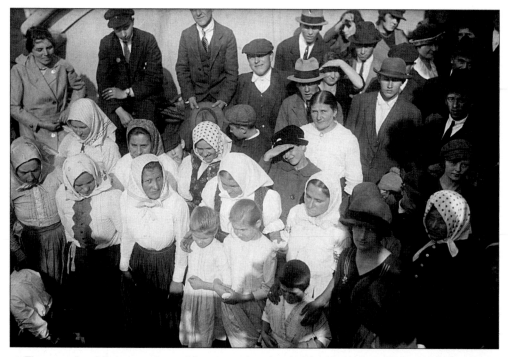

▲ Thousands of Poles, such as this group that landed in New York City, made the difficult to decision to leave their beloved homeland during the 1920s.

unpleasant, and foul smelling. Emigrants were allowed to come onto the deck during the day, but they were typically told to stay in the area behind the ship's smokestacks so that the better-paying passengers would not have to see them. Rather than getting fresh air, the emigrants breathed smelly, smoky air.

Those They Left Behind

Many Poles followed a pattern called chain migration, in which one member of a family made the trip first and then sent part of his or her wages back home to pay for another family member to come. Once that person made the journey, the added income meant the next family member could come that much more quickly.

Such, at least, was the plan—it worked well for many emigrant families, but not in all cases. If savings did not mount as quickly as hoped, husbands and wives became separated for longer periods of time. In some cases, husbands forgot their family obligations entirely and did nothing to bring over their wives.

Some adult children suffered a split with their families over the decision to stay in the United States rather than return to Poland. One Pole who made that decision wrote a letter saying that his mother asked him "with tears to come back to our country," adding, "My heart grieves at the words of my beloved mother."

Leaving After World War II

Large-scale emigration from Poland continued into the first few years after World War I. Then new U.S. immigration laws, passed in 1921 and 1924, largely shut it down.

After World War II, many Poles hoped to find safety and jobs in other countries. Some moved to Britain, but hundreds of thousands of British soldiers were also returning home and looking for work. Britain, for these and other reasons, was not welcoming. Many Poles decided to look to the United States.

The U.S. Congress passed laws in 1948 and 1950 that allowed larger than usual numbers of homeless Poles and Polish army veterans to come. Still, the demand for these opportunities was far greater than the number of people allowed to enter.

The situation in recent decades has not been so extreme. Immigration is not unlimited, but there are generally enough places available to meet the demand. Some Poles are finding ways around immigration laws. They come to the United States as students but then get jobs and stay beyond the time their student visas allow. Immigration officials estimated that in 2000, there were forty-seven thousand unauthorized Polish residents—those without visas or U.S. citizenship—in the United States. Many stay to earn money they can send back to Poland to help their families survive.

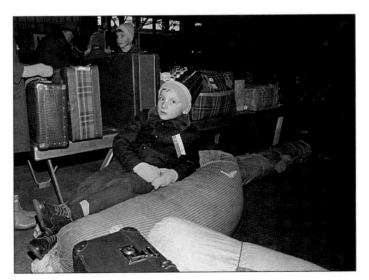

▶ A seven-year-old Polish boy waits at the port of Boston, Massachusetts, after arriving with his family in 1965. Many Poles who emigrated from the late 1940s to the late 1980s did so to escape the restrictions of communist rule in their homeland.

Arriving in the United States

Poles began arriving in what is now the United States in colonial times. These early arrivals were welcomed because they had valuable skills. The Polish immigrants who came after the mid-1850s, however, faced a different situation in their new home.

Poles in Jamestown

Jamestown, Virginia—the first permanent British colony in what is now the United States—was founded in 1607. The very next year, eight Polish workers arrived. Skilled in glassblowing (producing glassware and bottles) and making pitch (a substance made from pine tar often used to waterproof wooden ships), they had been invited to the new world to launch these industries. By the late 1610s, Jamestown had about fifty Polish residents.

▼ A wagon train of Polish immigrants arrives in White Deer, Texas, in about 1920. Polish American settlers came to Texas through the late 1800s and early 1900s because of the available farmland.

Later in the 1600s, other Poles settled in the Dutch colony of New Amsterdam (which became New York City) or in Pennsylvania. All of these early arrivals came as individuals or in small groups.

The Exiles of Failed Rebellions

Fond memories of the service of Tadeusz Kosciuszko and Kazimierz Pulaski in the American Revolution led Americans to eagerly offer a home to the 234 exiles of the failed 1830–1831 rebellion in Poland. Leading U.S. citizens formed a committee to help them find jobs and places to live when they arrived in 1834.

A few hundred more exiles joined this first group after another failed revolt in 1848. Some of these exiles grew unhappy in the unfamiliar society and moved on to other countries. Many of the exiles stayed in the United States, however. They married, learned English, and adapted to the ways of their new homeland. They settled mostly in the cities of the Northeast, from Boston, Massachusetts, to Washington, D.C., with the largest number in New York. They often became teachers or entered business.

Reaching Texas

The first Poles who came to the United States for economic reasons settled in Texas in the 1850s. They, too, were welcomed. The huge state of Texas was largely uninhabited by white people at the time, and most of the land was not yet cultivated. The immigrants came prepared, bringing farm tools and plows. They also carried with them the bell and cross from their village church.

"The arrival of the colony was one of the most picturesque scenes in my boyhood . . . . Some had on wooden shoes, and, almost without exception, all wore broad-brimmed, low-crowned black felt hats, nothing like the hats that were worn in Texas. They also wore blue jackets of heavy woolen cloth."

Texas writer L. B. Russell, recalling the Poles who settled in Texas in the 1850s

Ellis Island

The great mass movement of Polish immigrants started in the 1870s. Most of these immigrants passed through Ellis Island in New York Harbor, which was the government's main immigration station after 1892.

The first step in arriving—and the most frightening—was a medical inspection. Failing it meant being sent back to Poland. Only about 2 percent of all immigrants were sent back, but immigrants feared this stage, as the Polish Jewish writer Isaac Bashevis Singer later recalled: "So many immigrants, I remember, before they went to America, went to doctors to cure their eyes and all kinds of sicknesses which they suspected might hinder them of entering the United States."

The next step was being registered by an immigration agent. Agents asked the immigrants their names and ages; where they planned to settle; what relative, if any, they were joining; what their occupation was; and how much cash they had. Interpreters translated the questions and answers, which the agents wrote down.

The entire process could take as little as an hour, but the atmosphere was tense. The immigrants, tired and anxious, clutched their belongings in the crowded Registry Room, which was filled with hundreds of people and the sounds of many different languages. Most moved through quickly, but some were taken out of line

▼ As more and more immigrants arrived in the United States, the government imposed controls and inspections. This inspection card was issued to a Polish immigrant who left Danzig (now Gdansk), Poland, in 1925. The immigrant passed inspection in Poland but was hospitalized on arrival in the United States.

The Medical Exam at Ellis Island

Doctors quickly scanned the immigrants streaming into the main building at Ellis Island, looking for obvious physical problems. Using chalk, they wrote code letters on the clothes of anyone with a difficulty—"B" for bad back, "H" for heart condition, and so on. Using a hook, they pulled up each person's eyelids to look for signs of trachoma, an eye disease. People found to have trachoma were sent back. About half the immigrants were healthy enough to continue the admission process. Those with chalk marks were subjected to a closer examination. If doctors considered their injury or illness too severe, the hopeful immigrants had to return to Poland. Those with less serious problems stayed at Ellis Island's hospital until they were well.

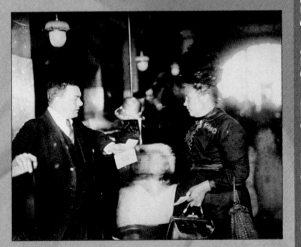

▲ Ellis Island inspectors chalked four letters on this immigrant's dress, just below her left shoulder. The letters tell the doctor (*left*) that she has various health problems.

because of illness, misunderstanding, or other problems. The stress was relieved only when the agent approved entry. Then the immigrants passed through the far end of the Registry Room and began the next stage of their journey.

Immigrant Status

When they entered the United States, Polish immigrants were given the status of resident aliens. They were not U.S. citizens, but they had the right to live and work in the United States and enjoyed freedom of speech and religion. After five years, they could apply to become U.S. citizens through the process called naturalization. To gain citizenship, immigrants had to be of "good moral character," swear allegiance to the United States, and pass a test. The test varied over time—the ability to read and write and the ability to speak English both became requirements.

From 1855 until 1922, female immigrants could become citizens by marrying a U.S. citizen. Immigrant children gained U.S. citizenship when their parents did. All children born in the United States, however, become U.S. citizens at birth.

New Jobs and Homes

Almost all of the Polish immigrants who came from the 1870s to the mid-1920s were skilled in farmwork, but few people had enough money to buy land when they reached the United States. They had to find work in other occupations. Luckily, they arrived at a time when U.S. industries were booming. Meatpacking plants, steel mills, and automobile factories needed strong, hardworking laborers. Immigrants—Poles and others—flocked to the cities of the Northeast and Midwest to help meet that need. Many who had been coal miners in Poland settled in the coal-bearing mountains of Pennsylvania and Ohio.

Laws Affecting Immigration

The huge increase in immigration from Europe that began in 1870 led to strong nativist feeling in the United States that grew out of prejudice. Protestants (the majority of Americans at the time) feared growing numbers of Polish and Italian immigrants would increase the influence of the Roman Catholic Church in the United States.

Polish immigrants were an easy target, since their appearance, customs, and language set them apart. Many news stories and books wrongly charged that immigrants lacked intelligence—claims that some Americans believed. Prejudiced Americans also falsely accused Polish immigrants of being loud and ignorant.

Growing opposition to immigration led Congress to pass a law in 1921 that put a limit on the number of immigrants. It also set up quotas based on the proportion of people from each country living in the United States in 1920. That decision meant fewer immigrants could enter from central, eastern, or southern Europe. Congress passed an even tougher law in 1924—known as the National Origins Act—that limited total immigration even further and set the quotas for countries in central, eastern, and southern Europe even lower.

The 1924 law drastically cut Polish immigration. Between 1918, when World War I ended, and 1924, nearly 250,000 people came to the United States from Poland. Throughout the 1930s, only about 17,000 Poles arrived in the United States.

Arriving After World War II

After World War II, nativist feelings faded, and Americans became willing to accept renewed immigration. The prejudiced attitudes toward Poles changed as Americans realized the extent of Polish

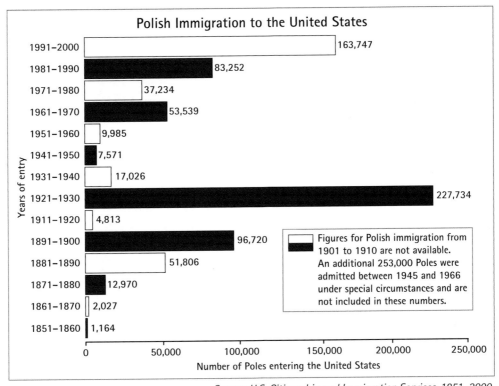

Polish Immigration to the United States

Years of entry	Number of Poles entering the United States
1991–2000	163,747
1981–1990	83,252
1971–1980	37,234
1961–1970	53,539
1951–1960	9,985
1941–1950	7,571
1931–1940	17,026
1921–1930	227,734
1911–1920	4,813
1891–1900	96,720
1881–1890	51,806
1871–1880	12,970
1861–1870	2,027
1851–1860	1,164

Figures for Polish immigration from 1901 to 1910 are not available. An additional 253,000 Poles were admitted between 1945 and 1966 under special circumstances and are not included in these numbers.

Source: U.S. Citizenship and Immigration Services, 1851–2000

▲ This chart shows how many Poles arrived in the United States between 1851 and 2000. Today, between ten and fifteen thousand Poles arrive every year.

suffering and bravery during the war. The Displaced Persons Act of 1948 and an additional law passed in 1950 allowed in Poles who had fought against Germany and large numbers of Polish civilians who had lost their homes. From 1945 to 1966, more than two hundred fifty thousand Poles came to the United States.

The newer immigrants, like the older ones, settled mainly in the Northeast and Midwest, but they did not necessarily integrate with the Polish American community that already existed. The two groups, with their very different experiences, remained distinct.

Congress finally dropped national quotas by passing the Immigration Act of 1965. That change again opened the door to large numbers of Polish immigrants. This wave of Polish immigration differed from that of the period from the 1870s to the 1920s. The new arrivals were generally well educated. Many were teachers or students; others found work as professionals, technicians, or artists. Many looked forward to the greater freedom of U.S. society. Like those who came immediately after World War II, they had little contact with the established Polish American community.

Polish Americans from 1850 to 1945

T he political exiles who came to the United States from Poland in the first half of the 1800s blended into the cities where they settled. They created some Polish organizations, but there were few of these immigrants, and they were scattered in many different cities. They did not have a large-scale impact on U.S. society. When immigrants began coming in greater numbers, however, Polish Americans created many lasting communities.

Living in Texas

Several hundred Poles settled in Texas beginning in 1854. A Polish Catholic priest, Leopold Moczygemba, was the inspiration behind their arrival. He had originally come to Texas in 1852 to serve German settlers there. Impressed by the growth of that community,

Leopold Moczygemba (1824–1891)

Father Moczygemba was born in southwest Poland and educated in Catholic schools before becoming a priest in 1847. The bishop of Galveston, Texas, was looking for priests to minister to Catholics in Texas, and Moczygemba agreed to go. He served German communities already there and encouraged the emigration of many Poles to the state. Moczygemba spent the latter half of his life in the areas of Syracuse, New York, and Detroit, Michigan, where he founded several more parish churches and built some schools. Among the schools was a seminary at Orchard Lake, Michigan, used for many decades afterward to train Polish Catholic priests. In 1974, Moczygemba's coffin was moved to Panna Maria, Texas, and reburied on the spot where Moczygemba had said the first mass for the 1854 immigrants.

▲ Priests gathered at the Church of the Immaculate Conception of the Blessed Virgin Mary in Panna Maria, Texas, in 1929 to celebrate the town's seventy-fifth anniversary.

he wrote letters encouraging Poles to emigrate there. When the first group of Poles arrived in 1854, Father Moczygemba bought land and helped organize the community, which they named Panna Maria (Polish for Virgin Mary). He also led them in building a permanent church.

Over the next few years, several hundred Poles arrived in Texas and started other settlements. The settlers made a living by farming or selling craft work. These communities never grew very large or influential in the state. The Poles kept mostly to themselves, seldom mixing with other Texan settlers. These communities did not enter the mainstream of Texas life until after World War II.

Living in the Cities

Chicago, Illinois, quickly became the largest Polish American community. In 1870, about 25 percent of the forty thousand Polish Americans lived in Chicago. By 1918, the city had ten times that number. Other cities with major Polish American populations were Buffalo and New York City, New York; Milwaukee, Wisconsin; Pittsburgh and Scranton, Pennsylvania; Cleveland, Ohio; and Detroit, Michigan. Still, Chicago so dominated the Polish American community that it was, in effect, the capital of Polonia.

Whatever city they lived in, Polish Americans clustered in ethnic neighborhoods with the parish church at the center. Polish American

▲ Like other immigrants of the early 1900s, Polish Americans formed communities and neighborhoods within large cities. Many Polish Americans lived in this neighborhood in Chicago, Illinois.

neighborhoods were scattered in several different areas of a city. The neighborhoods were not usually exclusively Polish, but rather comprised a mix of Poles and other immigrant groups. Each ethnic group formed its own local institutions.

At first, families had to crowd into small apartments to keep their costs as low as possible. Many of the apartments had poor plumbing and few windows. One goal that drove Polish Americans was that of owning their own home. They saw this, rather than education or a high-status job, as the measure of success. Many Polish Americans bought homes as soon as they could, taking in boarders if they needed help to meet house payments. Children also went to work at an early age to help their families meet payments. By 1930, more than two-thirds of the Polish Americans in Milwaukee, Wisconsin, owned their own homes. Rates of home ownership were similar among Polish Americans in other U.S. cities.

Working in the Factories and Mines

Polish Americans found work in mines, mills, and factories. Working in the factories meant hard labor, in brutal and dangerous conditions, for low pay. People often worked up to seventy-two hours per week—week in and week out—without vacations. Iron foundries and steel mills were hot, smoky, filthy places. They were also dangerous, with dozens of workers dying in accidents each year. Adding to the danger was the fact that what few signs there were warning about hazards were written in English, which most Polish Americans could not read. Textile mills had their own hazards. The machines that wove cloth were so noisy they caused workers to become deaf, and hazardous working environments caused workers to develop other health problems as well.

Wages for factory work were extremely low: $1.50 (which would be about $33 now) a day for twelve hours of work. Worse, if a piece of work was found to be defective, some pay was withheld even if the problem was caused by the raw materials.

Miners found problems similar to those of factory workers. Working hours were long, and the labor itself grueling and dangerous. From 1900 to 1920, more than twelve thousand miners died in coal mine accidents in Pennsylvania; a quarter of them were Polish Americans. Many Poles, however, endured poor conditions, discrimination, and hard labor in the United States in the hope that one day they would able to return home to an independent Poland.

Joining Unions

As the number of miners and industrial workers grew, they tried to form labor unions so they could force companies to pay better wages, shorten hours, and improve working conditions. Polish American workers took part in these efforts from the beginning,

▲ The textile mills of the Northeast offered work to many immigrants, including children. Work was dangerous and hours were long. This Polish American boy toiled in the spinning room of a textile mill in Anthony, Rhode Island, in 1909.

but the unions did not always welcome them. For years, the United Mine Workers (UMW) tried to keep immigrant miners out of the union. In 1897, the UMW finally gave in and recruited Polish American and other immigrant miners. Five years later, the union's ranks were large enough that it could stage its first successful strike. The early years of union activity, from the late 1800s to the early 1900s, were often marked by violent struggles between workers and companies. Polish Americans, like other groups, risked their lives trying to establish the right to unionize.

In 1938, the Congress of Industrial Organizations (CIO) was formed to organize unskilled factory workers. This opened the union movement to large numbers of workers who had been unable to join a union before. More than five hundred thousand Polish Americans took the opportunity to join the CIO in its first years.

The Lattimer Massacre

Relations between miners and mine owners were often hostile and sometimes broke out into violence. During the summer of 1897, tension grew in the mines of east central Pennsylvania. Immigrant miners—many of them Polish Americans—were angry that they were paid less than U.S.-born miners, and in early September, they staged strikes at several mines in the area. On September 10, 1897, a few hundred striking miners marched, unarmed, to the Lattimer Mine. They were met by about 150 armed men under the command of the county sheriff. A scuffle broke out, and the sheriff's men began firing into the crowd. When the firing stopped, 19 miners were dead and 36 more were wounded. About 24 Polish American miners were among the casualties.

Family Lives

Polish American family life followed patterns established in the homeland—with some changes. In many cases, parents, children, grandparents, aunts, uncles, and cousins all came to the United States, although not necessarily all at once. These extended families often lived in the same home or at least near each other. Families tended to be large, with many children, as had been the case in Poland.

Many Polish American women and girls worked outside the home—having the additional income was one way struggling immigrant families could survive. Work within the Polish American community was considered preferable to work outside it. Women helped run family

▲ Many children of immigrants worked instead of going to school. These young miners worked in a coal mine in South Pittston, Pennsylvania, in 1911.

stores, did laundry or sewing, worked as beauticians, and acted as paid letter readers and writers. Many joined the legions of people streaming into growing factories.

Tensions arose within some families over the sharing of resources. Some children, especially sons, did not wish to give their earnings to their parents. Another source of conflict was the fact that parents—working such long hours—often had little contact with their children.

Helping Each Other Out

Like other immigrant groups, Polish Americans formed groups known as mutual aid societies to provide assistance to each other. Many of these groups collected small fees and then made payments when a family was in need, particularly after the death of a member who had been a worker. Some of these groups were formed by women. The Polish Women's Alliance provided insurance and financial services and grew to have many members.

Two larger groups had broader goals. In 1873, Polish Catholic priest Father Theodore Gieryk founded the Polish Roman Catholic Union. Originally meant to include all Polish Americans, it developed a Catholic focus. It helped communities start Polish schools and libraries. Its rival, formed in 1880, was the Polish National

▲ Members dress in Polish costumes at a Polish National Alliance gathering in 1899. The Alliance aimed to help Polish Americans advance in U.S. society. Now an insurance company, the PNA continues to play a civic role by sponsoring educational and charitable grants.

Alliance (PNA), which had a nonreligious outlook. The PNA welcomed anyone, including Jews and people from other national backgrounds, who supported independent Poland. Both groups grew very large—with about two hundred thousand members each—and both groups were firm supporters of the movement for an independent Poland during World War I.

Many Polish Americans remained dedicated to their former homeland. They gave generously to families and villages in the old country. Between 1900 and 1906, people in just two Polish regions received nearly $70 million (worth about $140 billion today) from family members in the United States. During and after World War I, Polish Americans sent millions more dollars to Poland.

Polish Americans in the Catholic Church

Religion was central to the lives of Polish American Catholics. The Catholic Church in the United States, however, did not always welcome them. In the United States, the Catholic Church was dominated by Irish and German priests and higher officials. Church officials and worshipers from these groups treated Polish Catholics harshly and blocked the advancement of Polish priests.

Polish Americans were not willing to have their churches and their parish finances dominated by the largely Irish church authorities, and they responded by setting up their own parishes. They based their right to do so on a Polish tradition in which nobles gave land to found a parish and gained the right to name the parish priest. They also drew upon the principles of democracy that they saw as central to life in the United States.

The first Polish American parish was established in 1867 in Chicago, Illinois. Soon, Polish

Polish American Publications

The first U.S. Polish-language newspaper—*Echo of Poland*—was founded in 1863 in New York City. Many other publications followed. Some showed interest in Polish developments, while others focused on Polish Americans or had a religious, literary, or political emphasis. Some spread the views of groups, such as the Polish National Alliance. Buffalo, New York, Chicago, and other cities with large Polish American populations had several of these papers—both dailies and weeklies. In the 1930s, papers began to publish supplements in English in efforts to reach the U.S.-born audience.

▼ Polish Americans always tried to support the cause of freedom in Poland. This group of Polish Americans went to the White House in the early 1900s to ask President Woodrow Wilson to continue U.S. backing for Polish independence.

> "Should we Poles renounce today our rights and our national character given to us by God? Should we disinherit our souls, and deprive ourselves of independence, in order that we might please the Pope and the Irish bishops? No, never! If our nation has any mission in humanity's reach for higher goals, then it must also have its own distinct, Polish faith, its National Church, as all creative peoples of the world have."
>
> *Constitution of the Polish National Catholic Church, written in 1904*

parishes were founded in other cities. Across the nation, there were 75 Polish American parishes by 1880, 330 by 1900, and more than 750 by 1920. Polish Americans raised the money to build and decorate the churches. Although they struggled to earn money, they still gave generously. It was a matter of pride; each church stood as a symbol of its congregation.

Many Polish American Catholics, however, wanted more say in their own parishes. In the late 1890s, Franciszek Hodur, a priest in Scranton, Pennsylvania, insisted that church members should have control over the selection of parish priests. The Roman Catholic Church excommunicated him, but he continued to preach and to organize opposition to Catholic authorities. Under Hodur's leadership, several parishes joined in 1904 to form the Polish National Catholic Church (PNCC). The new church followed many Roman Catholic practices, but services were in Polish rather than Latin, and the pope was no longer considered head of the church. The PNCC also celebrated many Polish national holidays as feast days. The PNCC continues to thrive and serve many thousands of members.

◀ An aerial view of the mainly Polish American city of Hamtramck, Michigan, shows the prominence of the parish church in the community.

Other Polish Americans wanted to remain within the Catholic Church but have a voice in church decisions. In 1901, Polish American Catholics met in Buffalo, New York, to address these issues. They sent a demand to Church authorities to appoint Polish American bishops in areas with large numbers of Polish Americans. In 1908, a bishop of Polish descent was named for Chicago.

Going to School

Across the United States, Polish Americans set up parish schools alongside their parish churches. These were parochial (religious) schools in which students were taught mainly by nuns and in Polish. These schools were the major vehicle for the education of the children of Polish immigrants in the early 1900s. By 1914, nearly 130,000 Polish American children attended these schools.

The education in the early 1900s was not extensive. Children were taught to read and write, but only enough to get by in the ethnic community. Like many other working-class immigrant children of the period, Polish American children did not attend these schools past the eighth grade or so, when parents took them out of school so they could go to work. Since many families also had to pay tuition, finances played a large role in education. As family circumstances improved, Polish American children began attending school for more years.

Girls tended to lag behind boys in education. Polish American families saw little value in schooling for girls, who were expected to marry and raise families when they reached adulthood. Families also worried that girls who went to school into their teen years might be lured into sinful behavior.

The Polish American parish schools declined after the Great Depression began in 1929, bringing economic collapse to the United States. Polish Americans who lost their jobs and struggled to get by could no longer afford to send their children to the parish schools. Growing numbers of Polish American children then went to public schools. This helped speed their assimilation into U.S. culture.

"We all spoke Polish at home, so Polish was my only language until I went to school. I can still speak Polish. . . . I went to public school, but on Saturdays, like all kids in the neighborhood, I attended the Polish school. Then I was fluent in Polish."

U.S. Air Force General Donald J. Kutyna, the grandson of Polish immigrants, remembering his childhood in Chicago, Illinois, in the 1930s and 1940s

CHAPTER 5

Polish Americans from 1945 to Today

The later 1900s saw many changes in Polonia. Polish Americans joined other Americans in the migration of city dwellers to the suburbs that was taking place across the United States. They looked forward to owning larger houses with their own yards in cleaner, quieter, safer neighborhoods.

After the War

After World War II, the Polish American community changed its attitude toward education. Earlier generations had received less opportunity for schooling, but after World War II, Polish Americans tended to stay in school longer and go to college in increasing numbers. In the 1990s, about half of all Polish Americans between the ages of eighteen and twenty-four had some college education, and another 11 percent had earned a college degree.

Occupations changed as well, not just in the Polish community but among other immigrant groups of the same period and their descendants. By the 1990s, fewer Polish Americans worked in factories or mines. About one-third had management and professional jobs, and another third held technical, sales, and administrative jobs.

Politics and Ethnic Revival

Growing Polish American involvement in politics was another change that marked the postwar years. Immigrants and their children had focused on the struggle to survive. After World War II, however, the later generations—who had more education and were more Americanized—began to win political office. Edmund Muskie was elected as governor of Maine in the 1950s and later had a distinguished career in the Senate. In the late 1950s, as many as fifteen Polish Americans served in the House of Representatives.

The 1960s and 1970s also saw a revival of interest in Polish culture. One contributing factor was the influx of new immigrants, who had closer contact with contemporary Polish culture. Another was the growth to adulthood of the grandchildren of Polish immigrants. As they began to raise families, they wanted to learn more from their grandparents about Polish traditions.

▼ Polish Americans honor their heroes, heritage, and traditions in the 2004 annual Pulaski Day Parade held in New York City every March. The parade is named for Kazimierz Pulaski (1745–1779), the Polish military commander who died fighting for U.S. independence in the American Revolution.

"The Polish people have many beautiful traditions and customs just like any other nationality. If we do not preserve these customs and traditions from the past, then what do the present generation and future generations have to look for? We are really preserving this for our youth, for the future. If we don't preserve these things, they will be lost."

Joann Ozog, the daughter of Polish immigrants, on the importance of her work promoting Polish culture with the Polish Museum of America in Chicago, Illinois

> "Most likely to some people we are clannish, but this is for convenience sake. My father is eighty-seven years old and he never learned English. He never really adjusted to this country at all. If I have to take care of my parents, I might as well live next door to them. My brother . . . lives across the street. If I go on vacation, he can look after my parents."
>
> *Immigrant Wojtek Pobog, commenting in the late 1970s about Polish American society*

Relations with Other Americans

In the years after World War II, Polish Americans were sometimes the object of "Polish jokes," insults that made fun of them by playing on a false stereotype. Problems among ethnic and national groups decreased over time, however, especially as groups mixed. Around 1900, virtually all Polish Americans married other Polish Americans. Fifty years later, fewer than half of all Polish Americans married someone with the same heritage.

Differences and Similarities

The Polish American community changed as new immigrants arrived

▼ The majority of Polish immigrants and their descendants held fast to the Catholic faith. The National Shrine to Czestochowa in Doylestown, Pennsylvania, is dedicated to the Black Madonna. A statue of the beloved Pope John Paul II of Poland, who died in 2005, also marks the grounds.

In 1981, several thousand demonstrators gathered in Chicago, Illinois, to protest the Soviet Union's domination of Poland. Chicago is home to the largest Polish American community in the United States.

and as the descendants of earlier immigrants became adults. By 1990, more than 90 percent of Polish Americans had been born in the United States. Children and grandchildren of the people who had come in the early 1900s were members of Polonia, but they were also an integrated and significant part of U.S. society.

The new immigrants, on the other hand, had lived through very different experiences in Poland. Although many of them settled in the same cities where Poles had settled before, they did not move into the old ethnic neighborhoods. The two groups generally did not belong to the same organizations.

Polish Americans of all generations and backgrounds remained united in their support for an independent, free Poland. Both older and newer Polish Americans gave generously to support Solidarity and to help the Polish people through food shortages and economic problems. Another common thread in Polonia is the desire to keep Polish culture alive in the United States.

The Polish American Congress

Polish Americans joined together in 1944 to form the Polish American Congress. Its initial goal was to pressure the U.S. government to prevent domination of the Polish government by the Soviet Union after World War II. That goal failed when the U.S. government allowed the Soviets a free hand and agreed to give them some of Poland's territory. The Polish American Congress bitterly denounced these actions. In the 1980s, the Polish American Congress urged the U.S. government to support Solidarity.

Polish Americans in U.S. Society

In the 2000 Census, almost nine million people counted themselves as Polish Americans. Today, estimates put that figure closer to ten million.

The states with the largest Polish American populations are in the Northeast and Midwest—areas where Polish immigrants traditionally settled. Chicago, Illinois, remains the chief center of Polonia, with more than nine hundred thousand Polish Americans living in the city and its suburbs. Other cities with large Polish American populations include New York City, with about three hundred thousand, and Detroit, Michigan, which has about two hundred thousand.

Older Polish American neighborhoods have declined in several cities as Polish Americans moved to the suburbs. In some cases, Polish Americans have concentrated in the same suburb, basically

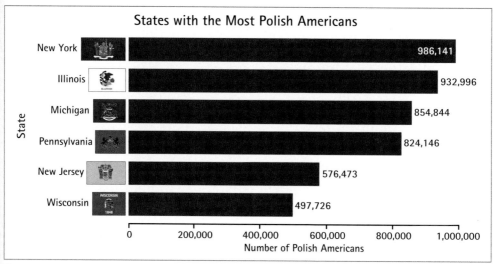

Source: U.S. Census Bureau, Census 2000

▲ This chart shows the states where most Polish Americans live. New York has the highest number of Polish Americans. The state with the highest percentage of Polish Americans (more than 9 percent of the population) is Wisconsin.

moving the ethnic neighborhood to a new location.

The educational and economic success of Polish Americans continues today. Polish Americans now have even higher levels of education than in the past. More of them hold professional, managerial, and other high-level jobs. Polish Americans remain an important force in the Roman Catholic Church and account for about one in five American Catholics.

The Idea of Polonia

With all the changes that have taken place in the last few decades, what has happened to Polonia? Many Polish neighborhoods are no longer there, and membership in Polish organizations, after reaching a high in the 1950s, has steadily declined. Only about one in eight Polish Americans speak Polish. Marriage outside the group has soared to more than 80 percent among Polish Americans. Surveys show that Polish Americans have little knowledge of issues that were once important to Poland.

"What helped me in life, I am sure, was being self-confident. It all came to me with my upbringing in a Polish family in Chicago close to my peers and close to my family."

U.S. Air Force General Donald J. Kutyna, whose many honors include the Defense and Air Force Distinguished Service Medals, Distinguished Flying Cross, and Air Force Commendation Medal

Despite these trends, a strong Polish American identity exists today. Many Polish parishes are thriving. Polish newspapers and magazines, which had once been published only in Polish, have become bilingual or are printed completely in English, but they are still circulating. Although Polish Americans have married people from other groups, they are still interested in maintaining traditions, such as sharing the oplatek on Christmas Eve. Many couples with mixed ancestry—for example, a Polish American man and an Irish American woman—teach their children about the traditions and cultures of both national heritages.

Polish Americans also maintain traditions by holding parades celebrating their heritage. Chicago holds a Polish Constitution Day Parade, celebrating the anniversary on May 3 of the Polish Constitution of 1791. The event has taken place since 1891. New York City has staged a Pulaski Day Parade every March since 1937.

▲ Kazimierz Jakubczak came to the United States in 1960. He works making Polish sausages in Milwaukee, Wisconsin, where there is a large Polish American community.

Polish food and music are a vital part of Polish American culture. Polish Americans and others enjoy kielbasa (Polish sausage); pierogi (packets of dough filled with potatoes and other ingredients); and *golabki* (stuffed cabbage leaves). Some Catholic parishes that are not Polish have adopted the sharing of oplatek on Christmas Eve.

Polish American music and dancing are greatly enjoyed in the United States. The polka originated in Bohemia (now part of the Czech Republic) but was adopted by Polish Americans. The traditional polonaise is a formal dance that was popular in Poland and is still practiced by Polish American dance companies.

Contributions of Polish Americans

Polish Americans have made numerous contributions to the United States. For many decades, miners in Pennsylvania have risked their lives and health in coal mines. Other Polish Americans have labored steel mills, auto factories, textile mills, glassworks, and countless other sites of U.S. industry. Cities such as Chicago, Buffalo, and Detroit—among many others—have been shaped by the hundreds of thousands of Polish Americans who lived in them.

Thousands of Polish Americans fought in wars, beginning with the American Revolution and continuing through World War I and World War II to the present day. Among these brave heroes were the Civil War general Wlodzimierz Krzyzanowski and Matt Urban, the most decorated American soldier in history.

Other individual Polish Americans have made wide-ranging and important contributions. Nobel Prize winners in the Polish American community include physicist Frank Wilczek, medical researcher Andrew Schally, and poet Czeslaw Milosz. Engineer Ralph Modjeski has been called "America's greatest bridge builder," while Mieczyslaw Bekker designed the Lunar Roving Vehicle used in NASA's Apollo Moon missions. Steve Wozniak, who helped develop the first Apple computers, was a major force in launching the personal computer industry.

▲ Polish American Steve Wozniak, co-founder of Apple Computer, was the designer of the first personal computer to sell in large numbers. His invention had a huge impact on people around the world.

The Entertainers

Pola Negri, a Polish actress who came to Hollywood in the early 1920s, became a noted silent film star. She has been followed by many other actresses of Polish heritage, including, in recent years, Leelee Sobieski. Behind the camera, brothers Larry and Andy Wachowski released the first of their hugely successful *Matrix* movies in 1999.

Polish American musicians have delighted audiences with a wide range of music. They include classical pianist Artur Rubinstein (a Polish Jew and devout Polish patriot), orchestra conductor Leopold Stokowski (who came to the United States in the 1930s), flamboyant entertainer and pianist Liberace, jazz performers Gene Krupa and Michael Urbaniak, and rock stars Mitch Ryder and Pat Benatar. Bobby Vinton, a singer called "the Polish prince," remains extremely popular with Polish Americans.

Polonia has produced many sports professionals, but Polish Americans stand out in baseball. Great baseball stars include Stan Musial, Al Simmons, and Carl Yastrzemski. In 2005, one-third of the starting line-up of World Series champions the Chicago White Sox was Polish American.

From the Jamestown colony to the present, people of Polish heritage have made a profound impact. Polish Americans remain justly proud of their people's many contributions to American life.

Notable Polish Americans

Pat Benatar (1953–) U.S.-born rock singer who studied opera and has won four Grammy Awards for vocal performance.

Zbigniew Brzezinski (1928–) Polish-born chief foreign policy adviser to President Jimmy Carter (1977–1981); was awarded the Presidential Medal of Freedom.

Erasmus Jerzmanowski (1844–1909) Polish-born philanthropist and engineer who played important roles in both the Polish American community and the early U.S. gas industry.

Wlodzimierz Krzyzanowski (1824–1887) Polish-born patriot who was colonel of the Polish Legion in the Civil War before being promoted to general by President Abraham Lincoln.

Stephanie Kwolek (1923–) U.S.-born scientist who created the strong synthetic fiber Kevlar and is one of the few women in the National Inventors Hall of Fame.

Liberace (1919–1987) U.S.-born son of a Polish immigrant mother and Italian immigrant father who became famous for his piano performances that mixed popular and classical music with showmanship.

Barbara Mikulski (1936–) U.S.-born social worker who entered politics in 1971 and served as a Congresswoman from Maryland before being elected to the U.S. Senate in 1986.

Czeslaw Milosz (1911–2004) Lithuanian-born Polish poet and essayist; immigrated in 1960 and won the 1980 Nobel Prize in Literature.

Stan Musial (1920–) U.S.-born professional baseball player; won seven National League batting titles and three Most Valuable Player awards.

John M. Shalikashvili (1936–) Polish-born solider who rose through the ranks to the military's highest ranking position, Chairman of the Joint Chiefs of Staff (1993–1997).

Matt Urban (1919–1995) U.S.-born military hero of World War II; won twenty-nine awards and medals.

Steve Wozniak (1950–) U.S.-born co-founder of Apple Computer and innovator in the field of personal computers.

Maria Zakrzewska (1829–1902) German-born Polish immigrant; founded the New England Hospital for Women and Children in Boston, Massachusetts.

Time Line

1608   Eight skilled Polish workers arrive in the colony of Jamestown, Virginia.

1772   Prussia, Russia, and Austria seize parts of Poland in the first partition.

1776   Tadeusz Kosciuszko arrives in North America.

1777   Kasimierz Pulaski arrives in North America.

1795   Partition of Poland by Prussia, Russia, and Austria results in the elimination of the Polish nation.

1830   Poles begin a revolt against foreign rule.

1834   Leaders of the failed 1830–1831 revolt arrive in the United States.

1848–1851   More exiles come to the United States after another failed revolt.

1854   Polish immigrants found Panna Maria, Texas.

1867   First Polish Catholic parish is established, in Chicago, Illinois.

1873   Polish Roman Catholic Union is founded.

1880   Polish National Alliance is founded.

1897   Miners at the Lattimer coal mine in Pennsylvania are massacred.

1904   Polish National Catholic Church is founded.

1908   Roman Catholic Church names the first Polish American bishop, in Chicago, Illinois.

1918   Poland gains independence and is recognized the following year.

1921   Congress passes legislation limiting immigration and putting quotas on the number of immigrants from each nation.

1924   Congress passes National Origins Act (also known as the Immigration Act of 1924) further limiting immigration and ending the main wave of Polish immigration.

1939   German troops invade Poland, launching World War II; Poland falls soon after and is divided between Germany and the Soviet Union.

1944   Polish American Congress is formed.

1945   Poland is liberated from German control; communists take control of the Polish government two years later.

1948   Congress passes the Displaced Persons Acts.

1965   Immigration Act puts an end to national quotas for immigration.

1966   Church dedicated to the Black Madonna of Czestochowa opens in Doylestown, Pennsylvania.

1978   Karol Wojtyla, a Polish cardinal, becomes Pope John Paul II.

1980   Solidarity rises in Poland; the government outlaws Soldiarity and declares martial law the next year.

1989   Free elections are held in Poland, leading to the collapse of communism.

2006   Polish Americans number an estimated ten million.

Glossary

alien person living in a nation other than his or her birth nation and who has not become a citizen of his or her new nation of residence

assimilation process of being absorbed into a new culture

boarder person who lives in the home of unrelated people, paying a monthly fee for rent and food

census official population count

communist person who follows the political system of communism, in which government has strong control and property is shared among all citizens

culture language, beliefs, customs, and ways of life shared by a group of people from the same region or nation

emigrate leave one nation or region to go and live in another place

ethnic having to do with people who come from the same country or region and share language and culture

excommunicate officially expel from membership in the Catholic Church

exile person who is forced or feels compelled to leave his or her homeland

heritage something handed down from previous generations

immigrant person who arrives in a new nation or region to take up residence

intellectual person who spends a lot of time studying and thinking

labor union organization, often in a particular trade or business, that represents the rights of workers

martial law rule of an area by the military, usually put in place as a temporary, emergency action

mutual aid society organization in which members of the group, who are usually from a common background, help each other and perform social services separately from government agencies or private businesses

nativist person who wanted limits placed on U.S. immigration to protect the power and position of white, U.S.-born Americans

naturalization process of becoming a citizen by living in the United States for a number of years and passing a citizenship test

parish area served by a single church

patriot person who shows loyalty and devotion to his or her homeland

peasant person of low social status who generally worked on farms

prejudice bias against or dislike of a person or group because of race, nationality, or other factors

quota assigned proportion; in the case of immigration, a limit on the number of immigrants allowed from a particular country

steerage section of a steamship that provided lower-class accommodations and was used by passengers who could not afford cabins

stereotype image, often incorrect, that people have of certain groups

visa document that permits a person to enter a nation for a set period of time

Further Resources

Books

Greene, Meg. *The Polish Americans.* Immigrants in America (series).
   Lucent (2004).

Kuniczak, W. S. *My Name Is Million: An Illustrated History of the Poles in
   America.* Hippocrene Books (1999).

Maass, Christel T. *Illuminating the Particular: Photographs of Milwaukee's
   Polish South Side.* University of Wisconsin Press (2003).

Raatma, Lucia. *Polish Americans.* Our Cultural Heritage (series). Child's
   World (2002).

Wallner, Rosemary. *Polish Immigrants, 1890-1920.* Coming to America (series).
   Blue Earth Books (2002).

Web Sites

Polish Internet
www.polskiinternet.com/english
Information on many aspects of Polish culture and heritage in the United States

Polish Roots
www.polishroots.com
Polish immigration, history, culture, and news

Publisher's note to educators and parents: Our editors have carefully reviewed these Web sites to ensure that they are suitable for children. Many Web sites change frequently, however, and we cannot guarantee that a site's future contents will continue to meet our high standards of quality and educational value. Be advised that children should be closely supervised whenever they access the Internet.

Where to Visit

Polish American Cultural Center
308 Walnut Street, Philadelphia, PA 19106
Telephone: (215) 922-1700; *www.polishamericancenter.org*

About the Author

Dale Anderson studied history and literature at Harvard University in Cambridge, Massachusetts. He lives in Newtown, Pennsylvania, where he writes and edits educational books. Anderson has written many books for young people, including a history of Ellis Island, published by World Almanac® Library in its *Landmark Events in American History* series.

Index